STEAM AHEAD! DIY FOR KIDS

Amazing Science/ Technology/ Engineering/ Art/ Math projects for kids between ages 4-10

Written by:
Sumita Mukherjee

 info@wizkids.club

 www.wizkids.club

Author	:	Sumita Mukherjee
Illustrator	:	Dzynpro
First Edition	:	December 2016, Canada

Library of Congress Control Number: 2016918350

Table of Contents

"Creativity is contagious, pass it on!"
Albert Einstein

This book is dedicated to my daughter and the children of today who are incurably inquisitive and amazing inventors.
If you like this book, don't forget to check out other books from the Wizkids Club
http://wizkids.club/books/

Introduction

STEM or STEAM is an acronym and stands for Science, Technology, Engineering, Art and Math.

STEAM aims to fuse these subjects into a unified learning model, instead of each subject being taught individually and separately at school or home. STEAM is based on real-life, practical projects, and their applications. The drive behind it is to get more engagement with these subjects, and make it relatable to the world around us.

STEAM AHEAD! DIY FOR KIDS introduces younger kids to the magic of electronics, making their own games and toys, printing, and understanding basic scientific principles. Most importantly kids will have a blast. The activities are broken up into their area of practical implementation: Party, Build, Toys, and Art.
Plus there is a BONUS: MATERIAL LIST to make it easier to plan and prepare.

Hope you get your hands busy and have fun building LED cards, dance pads, hand made soaps, bubble blowers, play-doh circuits, projectors, cloud lanterns, scribbling bots and more!

STEAM Relevance
This book has been created so that kids can learn more about the meaning and lessons behind the projects. Each project will have a "STEAM Factors" section, to make kids aware of the science and logic behind the activities.

Difficulty Level

All the projects are intended for ages 4 to 10; some activities can be adapted for younger kids and some for older ones with few changes. The activities have been scaled 1 to 5 based on the complexity of the project, with a 1 indicating the activity is quite simple while a rating of 5 means the activity is more complex.

Safety Note
Some of the projects need adult supervision due to the possible risks involved while using coin batteries, scissors, sharp tools, hot glue, and any other thing that can create a hazard.

PARTY

LED Card

Create a circuit on paper to light up reindeer's nose

MATERIALS:

Peel and stick copper tape

1 X 3 volt coin battery size, CR2032

LED light
Pencil
Scissors
Art supply as desired
Stiff paper for the card
Binder clip

Difficulty: ●●●

Estimated Time: 30 mins

STEAM Factors:
This project is a fun way to teach kids about circuits. Copper tape is like a wire; it conducts electricity. Circuits can be designed by connecting them correctly to LEDs, battery and copper tape. This project integrates engineering with design, and aesthetics.

Instructions:

1) Take one coin cell battery and place it near the corner of the paper card. Fold the corner so that the paper can cover the battery.

2) Draw a circle around the battery and another one on the folded ear.

3) Take the copper tape and place it as shown. It should start from the center of the first circle and end in the second. There should be a gap to insert the LED.

4) Twist and bend the LED legs and place each leg under the copper tape as shown.

5) Place the battery on the circle and fold over the corner. Now take the binder clip and let it grab down the battery. The LED lights up!

6) Put another page over it and design it, as shown. You need to poke the LED through the front cover so that it sticks out. You can decorate the card as you please. I made a reindeer's nose shine!

Pop-Up Card

Make a pop-up card using paper

Instructions:

1) Take one paper and fold it into half like a card.

2) Make 6 cuts (1 inch long) on the creased side of the card. The center two slits can be slightly longer (1.5 inches) than the other ones. Fold the card and bend the slits up.

3) Open the card and push the slits into the card to make them pop out. It forms a box that sticks to the card.

4) Close the card and press the box flat. Open the card and check that the box pops up.

5) Now cut out your favorite designs and stick them to the pop up box.

6) Glue the 2nd colored paper at the back of this card. Your festive pop-up card is done!

MATERIALS:
2 Colorful Papers
Christmas or other cut outs
Scissors
Glue

Difficulty: ●

Estimated Time: 20 mins

STEAM Factors:
Paper bends along the line of weakness. In this project when the paper is folded, the creased line is the line of weakness. Make amazing pop-up cards using this science.

LED Necklace

Create light up jewelry using clay and LEDs

MATERIALS:
3 LEDs
3 x 3 volt coin battery size, CR2032
Air-dry clay
Quick dry paint
Old necklace
Thread or string
Stiff paper
Hot glue gun
Scissors

Difficulty: ●●●

Estimated Time: 30 mins

STEAM Factors:
Air-dry clay and LEDs lights are a perfect way to blend aesthetics with engineering. Have fun making ornaments and add a little bling with light!

Instructions:

WARNING: Coin cell batteries are dangerous when swallowed. ADULT SUPERVISION REQUIRED.

1) Take one LED and one coin cell battery. Touch the ends of LED to the battery so that the LED glows. If it doesn't light up, flip the battery and try again. It should glow once the positive end of the battery is in contact with the negative leg of the LED. This makes a circuit complete.

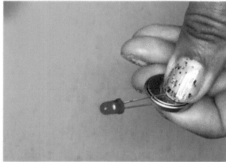

2) Now twist the legs of the LED so that they remain in contact with the battery. Using the tape, secure the circuit. The LED should keep on glowing.

3) Take some air-dry clay and cover the battery with it. This will be the centerpiece of the flower.

4) Take blobs of clay and press down to make 9-10 petals. Add petals to the centerpiece to make a flower. Use the hot glue gun to secure the petals to the centerpiece.

5) Color the flower and let it dry. Make two more flowers in a similar way.

6) Make a stiff flower base by cutting out floral shapes on stiff paper. Color them and let it dry. The stiff base is to attach the flowers so that we don't have to run the thread through the clay petals.

7) Glue the base to the LED clay flower. Follow the same process for the other two flowers.

8) Add a string to the flower base and tie them to the necklace band. Your glowing necklace is ready.

Balloon Drum

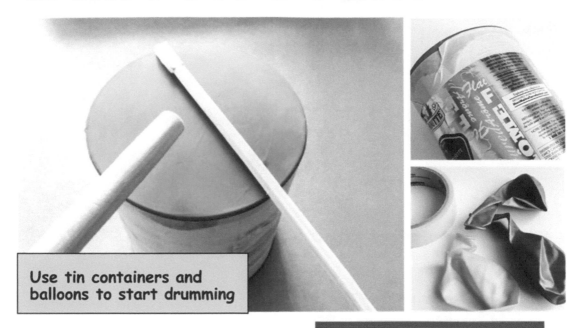

Use tin containers and balloons to start drumming

Instructions:

1) Blow the balloon so that it becomes stretchable.

2) Let the wind out of the balloon and cut the long nose of the balloon.

3) Stretch the balloon to fit to the mouth of the coffee tin as shown.

4) Secure balloon to the coffee tin with tape to make the drum.

5) Decorate the body of the drum with paint, stickers and embellishments.

6) Use the sticks to start drumming.

MATERIALS:
1 Empty coffee tin
1 Balloon
Tape
2 Sticks
Scissors
Drum decorating materials

Difficulty: ●

Estimated Time: 20 mins

STEAM Factors:
This musical instrument is an exciting way to teach kids about sound. The sound of each drum depends on the size of the container, the material it is made of, and the sizes and brands of balloons that are used.

Light-up Dance Pad

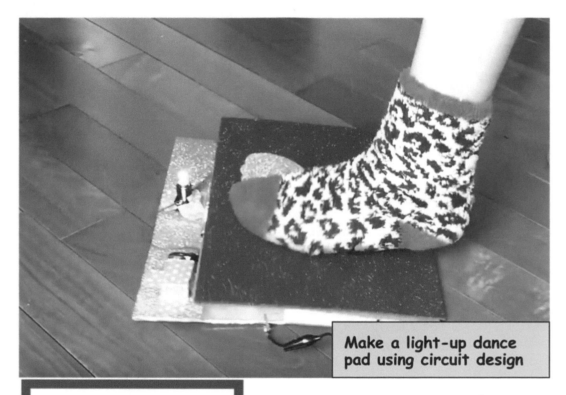

Make a light-up dance pad using circuit design

MATERIALS:
1 cardboard: 20 x 12 inches
Aluminum foil
1 x 9V Battery with wire cable connectors
1 toilet paper tube
1 light bulb with socket
2 alligator clips
Hot glue or tape
Reflective or shiny paper
Scissors

Difficulty: ●●●●

Estimated Time: 30 mins

STEAM Factors:
This project is a fun way to help kids understand circuits. Make your own dancing pad and enjoy every moment the circuit is complete and the bulb lights up!

Instructions:

WARNING: Using circuits and electrical connections can be dangerous. ADULT SUPERVISION IS REQUIRED.

1) Take the cardboard and fold it in such a way so that 2 inches or 5 cm remains jutting out. This will be the pad.

2) Attach an aluminum strip on the larger side of the cardboard as shown.

3) Add a strip of shiny paper on the jutting out part of the cardboard.

4) Cover the toilet paper tube with aluminum foil.

5) Glue the aluminum covered toilet paper tube on the inner flap of the dancing pad. It should make connection with the aluminum strip when the flap is closed. Ensure it doesn't touch the shiny paper. This will be the switch for the dance pad.

6) Put the battery and the light bulb on the shiny paper as shown. Secure with tape or hot glue gun.

7) Connect the battery to the wire.

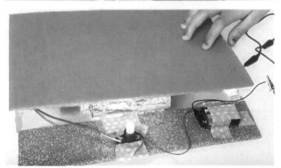

8) Take one alligator clip and use it to connect the wire from the battery to the aluminum strip on the cardboard as shown.

9) Take the second alligator clip and connect one end to the light bulb and the other end to the aluminum toilet paper tube.

10) When you close the lid, the bulb should light up. You can decorate your dance pad as you please.

BUILD

Squishy Circuit

Make a butterfly with Play-Doh using LEDs and Battery

Difficulty: ●●○

Estimated Time:
30 mins

STEAM Factors:
Do you love Play-Doh? You will love it even more when you discover how to bring it to life with LED lights. Add a new dimension to your creations with clay circuits and electricity.

MATERIALS:
2 Colorful Papers
Christmas or other cut outs
Scissors
Glue

Instructions:
WARNING: Electrical circuits can be dangerous. ADULT SUPERVISION REQUIRED when using it.

1) Make 2 balls of Play-Doh. Connect one ball to the (red) alligator clip and another ball to another (black) alligator clip. Now connect the alligator clips to the 9V battery.

2) Insert one leg of the LED to one ball and the other leg to the other ball of Play-Doh. The LED bulb should light up. If it doesn't, try flipping the LED legs and try again. Ensure the balls do not touch one another.

3) Play-Doh is a good conductor of electricity. The electric current passes from the battery, through the alligator wires to the Play-Doh and then to the LEDs. Hence the LEDs light up.

4) Use modeling clay to make the body of the butterfly and place it in between the wings. Since it is a bad conductor of electricity, it lets the electric current pass through the Play-Doh to the LEDs.

5) Decorate your butterfly as you please.

Shoebox Projector

Make a home projector with shoebox and magnifying glass

MATERIALS:

1 Shoebox
1 magnifying glass
Smart phone
Sharp knife
Tape
Play-Doh
Markers

Difficulty: ●●●

Estimated Time: 30 mins

STEAM Factors:
Understand the science behind light and lens as you make your own projector.

Instructions:

WARNING: Using a knife to cut the shoebox can be dangerous. ADULT SUPERVISION REQUIRED.

1) Open the lid of the shoebox and position the magnifying glass at the center of one of the shorter sides of the box. Use a marker to trace around it.

2) Now cut out an exact hole using the sharp knife. Ask an adult for help if required.

3) Take the magnifying glass and place it on the hole. Secure it with tape.

4) Set your phone to the highest brightness and lock the screen.

5) Take the smart phone and place it inside the shoebox upside down. The images formed on the wall will be inverted by the magnifying glass.

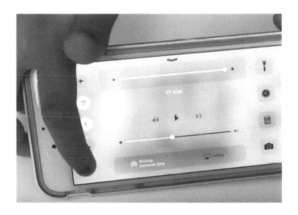

6) Move the smartphone back and forth to find what the right distance is for the magnifying glass to form the sharpest image on the wall.

7) Create a base for the phone using Play-Doh.

8) Now close the lid and your shoebox projector is ready. Play any movie or project photos from the phone onto the wall or a screen.

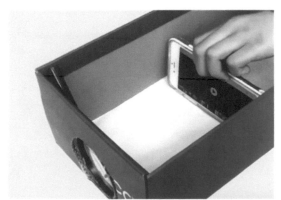

Gel Notebook

Make squishy notebook with liquids

Difficulty: ●●

Estimated Time:
20 mins

STEAM Factors:

Mix hair gel, oil and glitters and see what happens. An amazing way to teach kids about liquids that don't mix.

MATERIALS:

Ziplock bag
Notebook
Sticky-back glitter paper
Baby oil
Hair gel
Glitters
Food coloring
Tape
Scissors

Instructions:

1) Put some hair gel into the bag. Add some baby oil and glitter. Zip the bag closed once you have finished.

2) Take the notebook and place the zip gel bag on the hard cover page. Tape it to the cover so that it doesn't move.

3) Take the sticky back paper and cut out a square so that the zip gel bag is visible.

4) Stick it on top of the bag.

5) Your squishy notebook is ready!

Cloud Lantern

Make a glowing cloud

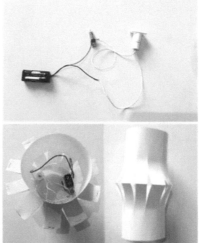

Difficulty: ●●●

Estimated Time: 20 mins

STEAM Factors:

Floating clouds that glow can be awesome. Build them on your own using circuits. Cool way to introduce kids to design and engineering

MATERIALS:

Paper lantern

Cotton batting

2 AA batteries with wire connector

Switch with wires

Bulb with socket

Tape

Hot glue gun

Instructions:

WARNING: Connecting wires and building a circuit can be dangerous. ADULT SUPERVISION REQUIRED when using it.

1) Connect one wire from the batteries to the switch. Connect the switch wire to the light bulb.

2) Take the second wire from the batteries and connect it to the light bulb. The bulb should glow when the switch is on as the circuit is complete.,

3) Cut out a paper lantern as shown and tape in the circuit carefully.

4) Take the cotton batting and hot glue it around the paper lantern. It should look like clouds. Now hang it up!

Lava Pen

Lava pen made of liquids that don't mix

Difficulty: ● ●

Estimated Time:
20 mins

STEAM Factors:

Mix water, oil, and glitter and see what happens. An amazing way to teach kids about liquids that don't mix.

MATERIALS:

Transparent PVC pipe

Baby oil

Pen as wide as the

transparent pipe.

Glitter

Water

Hot glue gun

Food coloring

Instructions:

WARNING: Hot glue gun can be dangerous. ADULT SUPERVISION REQUIRED when using it.

1) Unscrew the mouth and the back cap of the pen. Take out the ink refill stick. Fill the mouth of the pen with lots of hot glue. Stick the ink refill and hold it straight. Let it dry. This is the front piece.

2) Take the pipe and apply some glue on the inner part. Quickly stick in the front piece of the pen. Press it in and let it dry. It should be leak proof.

3) Once the glue has dried, pour colored water into the transparent pipe with a syringe. Fill it about half way. Add the glitter in.

4) Now suck some baby oil into a syringe and fill the rest of the pen.

5) Cover the back opening with the end cap of the pen.

6) Now give it a quick shake and see the glittery bubbles swim around.

TOYS

Paper Snakes

Make a paper snake by folding paper

Difficulty: ●●

Estimated Time: 20 mins

STEAM Factors:
Recycle paper towel tubes and learn the art of folding paper to make paper snakes. Design and aesthetics put together..

Instructions:

1) Cut out mouth shape from the toilet roll and paint it up.

2) Start the snake's the body by applying glue on the ends of the two contrasting strips of construction paper. Place them at a right angle.

3) Fold the bottom strip over the top strip, making sure they remain perpendicular. Crease the fold. Continue crisscrossing bottom over the top, keeping the strips at right angles to each other. It should become like a long spring.

4) Staple multiple long spring bodies to make it longer.

5) Staple the mouth. Add eyes, fangs and a tongue.

MATERIALS:

Toilet paper tube
Construction paper
cut in 1-inch
wide strips
Painting supplies
Embellishments like
googly eyes
Scissors
Glue
Stapler

Sling Shot

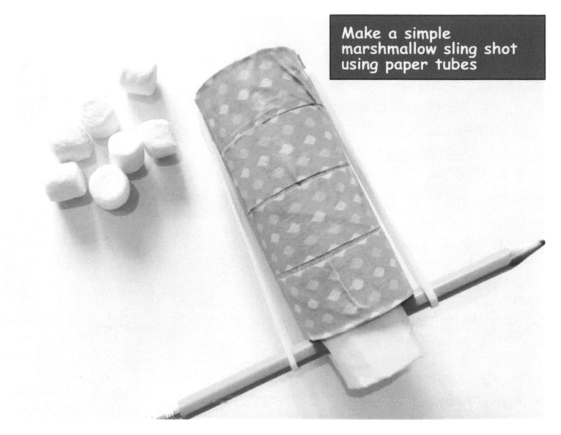

Make a simple marshmallow sling shot using paper tubes

MATERIALS:
2 toilet paper tubes
2 elastic bands
1 pencil
Colorful tape
Scissors
Mini marshmallows

Difficulty: ●●

Estimated Time: 20 mins

STEAM Factors:
Understand the concepts of energy in this fun project. How stored energy gets converted to motion energy.

Instructions:

1) Take one toilet paper tube, cut it into half lengthwise and tape it so that it becomes half the size of the original diameter. Tape it yellow.

2) Tape and decorate the 2nd tube.

3) Take the second orange tube and cut two slits as shown. Repeat it on the opposite end of the tube. Add 2 elastic bands as shown.

4) Take the 1st yellow tube and punch 2 holes. Insert the pencil through the holes as shown.

5) Assemble the blaster by sliding the smaller yellow tube into the larger orange one.

6) Hook each elastic band around a pencil end.

7) Load the mini marshmallows. Your slingshot is ready!

8) Hold the pencil with your fingers and pull down the elastic band. Take aim and let it go!

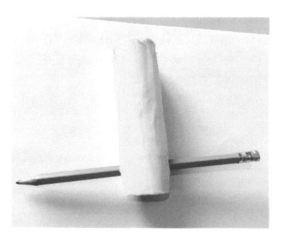

Bubble Blower

Recycle old bottles to make bubble blower

Difficulty: ●●

Estimated Time: 20 mins

STEAM Factors:

Recycle bottles to make bubble blowers. Soap and water hold air to form bubbles.

Instructions:

WARNING: Using a knife to cut the shoebox can be dangerous. ADULT SUPERVISION REQUIRED.

1) Take the bottle and cut it into half. You might ask an adult for help with this.

2) Cut out some mesh. Tape the mesh to the open side as shown.

3) Dilute the soap by adding little water.

4) Dip the bottle into the diluted liquid soap and blow into the mouth of the bottle to create bubbles.

MATERIALS:
1 empty bottle
Liquid bubble soap
Tape
1 mesh fruit bag or any mesh
Scissors

Scribbling Bot

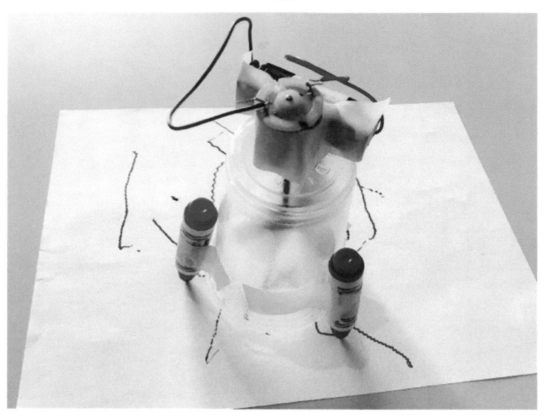

MATERIALS:

1 plastic cup
3 markers
1 motor
1 pencil battery with battery holder or 9V battery with 2 alligator clips
Straw
1 ink refill tube
1 nail
Tape

Difficulty: ●●●●●

Estimated Time: 30 mins

STEAM Factors:

Fun way to make a cup move by using motors. Engineering and science put together.

Instructions:

WARNING: Electric connection and a running motor can be dangerous. ADULT SUPERVISION REQUIRED.

1) Take the plastic cup and tape the 3 markers as shown. These would be like legs for the cup.

2) To make the fan for the motor we need the refill, straw and a nail. Cut a small piece of refill (2 inches long) and keep aside. Take the straw and cut out 2 pieces (1.5 inches long) from there. Nail in the 2 pieces of straw to the ink refill as shown.

3) Make a hole on top of the cup.

4) Insert the motor from the top and the fan from inside. Push them in together.

5) Tape the motor and battery to the top of the cup.

6) Take the battery and connect it to the motor with the wires. The motorized coloring machine is in action! Put a paper under it and it is ready to scribble!

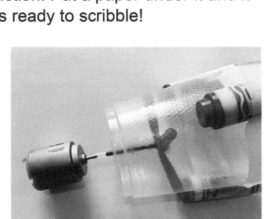

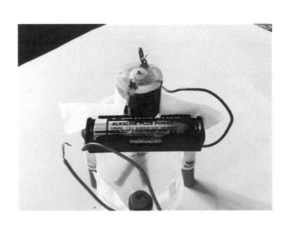

Cup and Ball

Difficulty: ●●

Estimated Time: 20 mins

STEAM Factors:

Understanding the curve or bend of a ball's path when tied to a string. Fun with science of motion and force.

Instructions:

1) Use colored tape to decorate the cup.

2) Make a hole at the bottom of the cup and run the yarn through it.

3) Tie the ball or bead to one end of the yarn. Knot the other end so that it doesn't pass through the hole. You can hot glue the yarn to the cup hole.

4) Pierce the stick through the cup as shown using scissors. Hot glue the stick so that it doesn't move or turn. Decorate it.

5) Now try to swing the ball and flip it into the cup. It is not as easy as it looks. Give it a shot!

MATERIALS:

1 plastic cup

1 stick

20 inches long yarn

Heavy bead or ball

Colored tape

Scissors

Hot glue

ART

LEGO Printing

Make tall towers and buildings using lego

Instructions:

1) Look at some real life building and decide which skyscraper you want to print.

2) Pour paint on the paper plate.

3) Dip the Lego into the paint and then stamp it onto the paper. Experiment with printing using both sides of the blocks and find out which side has circles and which creates squares or rectangles.

4) Keep experimenting to build building of various heights, width, and structure.

Difficulty: ●
Estimated Time: 20 mins

STEAM Factors:
Combine art and math to understand how construction of building takes place.

MATERIALS:

LEGO blocks

Paint

Paper plate

Colorful paper

Handmade Soap

Make handmade soaps from glycerine soap bars

Instructions:

WARNING: Melting soap in the microwave can be dangerous. ADULT SUPERVISION REQUIRED.

1) Put the glycerin soap in the glass cup and melt it in the microwave.

2) Add few drops of fragrance and color.

3) Carefully pour it into the ziplock bag and add the buttons or other embellishments.

4) Once cool, peel off the plastic bag to reveal your soap. You can use molds to make different shapes and sizes.

Difficulty:

Estimated Time: 20 mins

STEAM Factors:

Combination of science and art. Check out how heat can make a soap melt which can be remolded into different kinds of shapes.

MATERIALS:

Clear glycerin soap

Soap color

Fragrance (Optional)

Buttons and other em-bellishments

Glass cup

Ziplock bag

Absorption Art

Make decorative paper leaves

Instructions:

1) Take the filter papers together and cut out leaf patterns

2) Make doughnut rings in the middle of the paper as shown.

3) Fold the leaf three times making a point in the middle.

4) Carefully dip the tip of the point in the water. The water should start travelling up and spread the color throughout the paper.

5) Remove the leaf and hang it to dry.

6) Once dry, open it carefully to see how water travels through the leaves towards its ends.

Difficulty: ●●

Estimated Time: 20 mins

STEAM Factors:

Science of water travelling through paper and spreading it towards the tips.

MATERIALS:

6-7 coffee filter papers

Markers

Cup of water

Scissors

Refraction of light

Which way are the eyes looking: left or right?

Instructions:

1) Draw a face with eyes looking towards the left.

2) Take a glass of water and look through the glass. Which way do the eyes seem to look now?

3) Get creative and check how refraction of light changes the look of the sketch. Experiment more and find out how the size, direction of the image changes with various shapes of glass and distance from the image.

Difficulty: ●●
Estimated Time: 20 mins

STEAM Factors:
Have fun understanding the science behind refraction of light. When it passes through a glass of water, it inverts the image, like a magnifying glass.

MATERIALS:

1 glass of water
Drawing book
Pen

Spinning Color

Spinning wheel which makes 2 colors seem as one

Instructions:

1) Take the cardboard and cut out a circle.

2) Take the white paper and cut two circles of the same diameter by tracing around the cardboard.

3) Fold the paper circle into 8 equal parts. This is done by folding the circle in half, then fold the semi-circle again and then once more to get 8 equal parts.

4) Color each of the 8 parts alternatively: red-yellow on one paper circle and blue- yellow on the other paper.

5) Stick one to each side of the circle cardboard.

6) Run the thick string and spin it! Red-yellow spins to become one single color-orange. Blue-yellow spins to become green in color.

Difficulty: ●●
Estimated Time: 20 mins

STEAM Factors:

Understanding the science behind color mixing. 2 colors can blend to become one when spun fast.

MATERIALS:
Cardboard

White paper

Crayons

Scissors

Glue

Thick string

MATERIAL LIST FOR
STEAM AHEAD! DIY FOR KIDS

Cotton batting
Copper tape
Led lights
3v batteries
AA batteries
9v batteries
Binder clips
Air dry clay
Empty plastic bottles
Empty tin bottle
Plastic cups
Balloons
Cardboard
Construction paper
Color paper
Sticky-back paper
Shiny reflecting paper
Aluminum foil
Alligator clips
Cable connectors for battery or switch
Play-Doh
Modeling clay
Shoebox
Magnifying glass
Ziplock bags
Hair gel
Baby oil
Toilet paper tube

Paper plate
Glycerin soap
Soap color
Fragrance
Soft stuffing
Elastic bands
Pencils
Scissors
School glue
Glue stick
Hot glue gun
Colored tape
Knife
Markers
Notebook
Food coloring
Glitter
Pens
Switches
PVC transparent pipes
Mesh bags
Motors
Pen ink refill stick
Nails
Sticks
Beads and balls
Yarn
Lego blocks
Coffee filter papers
Stapler

Keiko, Kenzo and Eji are on their way to China with their school friends and a strict teacher. They visit the Forbidden Palace and discover that it is haunted. Strange things happen in the guesthouse. When they investigate, they are shocked to see an unearthly hollow face! Kenzo, being a brave heart, finds a clue and decides to get to the bottom of the mystery.

The book also offers insights and information on culture, history and geographic sites including the Great Wall of China, The Forbidden Palace, Zodiacs and Wonders of the World. It is a thrilling adventure book woven with real world facts, to make learning absolutely enjoyable. Science and technology has been fused into the story to inspire kids to explore and invent.

BUY NOW:

http://wizkids.club/ghost-of-the-forbidden-city/

Keiko, Kenzo and Eji are in the bustling city of Singapore to attend their cousin sister, Kiara's recital on Ancient Sea Trade. Keiko and Kiara discover a hidden note in an ancient urn, leading them into an acient treasure hunt. Soon they realise evil treasure hunters are out to get them. Find out what happens in this race that takes place under the South China Sea.

The book highlights the attractions of the city of Singapore. Facts on Maritime Silk Road, Singapore Flyer, Ancient Trade and famous shipwrecks in the world have been woven into the story so readers get a true sense of Singapore as they travel with our heroes in a dangerous undersea race for buried treasure.

BUY NOW:
http://wizkids.club/sunken-treasure-hunt/

This book encourages comprehensive learning for young kids. It is scientific, informative and creative.

It is about water cycle stages, and it increases understanding of scientific vocabulary and concepts. This book gives complete understanding of the water cycle through hands on learning and activities.

A fun activity book filled with quizzes, facts, information, illustration, sorting, question-answer key and various other activities.

-Comprehensive learning

-Growing imaginative and creative skills

-Developing memory

-Experimenting

-Generating ideas and stimulating the whole brain.

-STEM learning and scientific education

BUY NOW:
https://www.teacherspayteachers.com/Product/WATER-CYCLE-Hands-on-activity-and-learning-2585949

Seasons, day and night, senses, life cycles, plants. This unit encourages children to play independently. It promotes planning, preparation and execution of events like going on a holiday and inculcates leadership skills. It helps them understand concepts of life cycle, seasons, and senses as well. A fun activity book filled with quizzes, facts, information, illustration, sorting, question-answer key and various other activities.

-Comprehensive learning

-Growing imaginative and creative skills

-Developing memory

-Experimenting

-Generating ideas and stimulating the whole brain.

-STEM learning and scientific education

BUY NOW:
https://www.teacherspayteachers.com/Product/Scientific-Investigation-1831131/

This unit encourages children to play independently. It promotes planning, preparation and execution of events like hosting a birthday and inculcates leadership skills.

Awesome project ideas and fun learning these:

Science,
Math
Literacy
Games
Arts and crafts.

BUY NOW:

https://www.teacherspayteachers.com/Product/I-Can-Organise-My-Own-Birthday-1831125

This unit encourages children to play independently. It promotes planning, preparation and paper craft. Writing letters, memory games and reasoning tasks. Best for Prek-1. One in all pack!
Awesome project ideas and fun learning these:

Science,
Math
Literacy
Games
Arts and crafts.

BUY NOW:
https://www.teacherspayteachers.com/Product/MAKE-Paper-Fairies-and-Story-Books-1831110/

Join the

WIZKIDS CLUB

Enter today and win a FREE BOOK!

Do you have any travel adventure stories or project ideas you want share with me? Yes? Great! You can mail me at my id and become a member of the WIZKIDS CLUB!

www.wizkids.club

Write to me at: info@wizkids.club

CPSIA information can be obtained
at www.ICGtesting.com
Printed in the USA
LVHW071702070619
620218LV00038B/238/P